Pebble® Plus

EXPLORE LIFE CYCLES

An Apple Tree's Life Cycle

Mary Dunn

raintree
a Capstone company — publishers for children

Raintree is an imprint of Capstone Global Library Limited, a company incorporated in England and Wales
having its registered office at 264 Banbury Road, Oxford, OX2 7DY – Registered company number: 6695582

www.raintree.co.uk
myorders@raintree.co.uk

Edited by Anna Butzer
Designed by Kyle Grenz
Picture research by Wanda Winch
Production by Kathy McColley
Originated by Capstone Global Library Ltd

ISBN 978 1 4747 4332 7 (hardcover)
21 20 19 18 17
10 9 8 7 6 5 4 3 2 1

ISBN 978 1 4747 4338-9 (paperback)
22 21 20 19 18
10 9 8 7 6 5 4 3 2 1

British Library Cataloguing in Publication Data
A full catalogue record for this book is available from the British Library.

Acknowledgements
We would like to thank the following for permission to reproduce photographs: Dreamstime:
Deepspacedave, 7; Shutterstock: Adriana Nikolova, 21, branislavpudar, 19, gorillaimages, 13,
Helga42, 15, images72, back cover, 5, Michaela Steininger, cover, Nikohm Kedban, 3, 6, 8, 12, 24,
Nosyrevy, 10, 14, November Oscar Kilo, 17, Robert Schneider, 11, Zoom Team, 1; Thinkstock:
iStockphoto/Forester_, 9

Every effort has been made to contact copyright holders of material reproduced in this book. Any omissions will
be rectified in subsequent printings if notice is given to the publisher.

All the internet addresses (URLs) given in this book were valid at the time of going to press. However,
due to the dynamic nature of the internet, some addresses may have changed, or sites may have changed
or ceased to exist since publication. While the author and publisher regret any inconvenience this may
cause readers, no responsibility for any such changes can be accepted by either the author or the publisher.

Printed and bound in India.

Contents

Planting seeds in spring

Apples are a delicious, juicy fruit.

Yum! They grow on trees.

There are about 7,500 kinds

of apple trees.

5

Many apple trees start as tiny seeds.

After the seed is planted,

roots grow. Next, a shoot

pushes up out of the ground.

Leaves begin to grow.

The shoot becomes a seedling.

In two years, the plant is a sapling.

It is stronger and its trunk is getting thick.

A Red Delicious apple tree is fully grown in 6 to 10 years. An adult tree can grow to be 7.6 metres (25 feet) tall. Each spring, bright blossoms grow with the leaves.

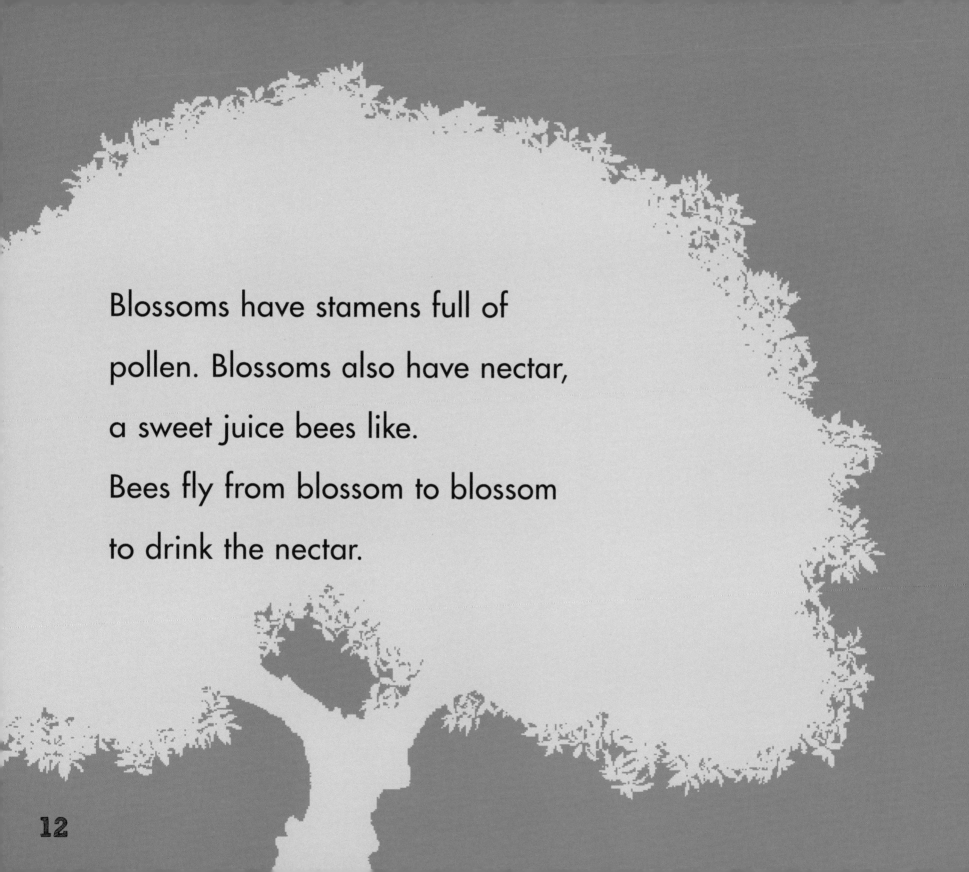

Blossoms have stamens full of pollen. Blossoms also have nectar, a sweet juice bees like.

Bees fly from blossom to blossom to drink the nectar.

Pollen dust sticks on bees' hairy legs. They carry it from one blossom to another. Pollen helps to make new apple seeds.

Growing fruit in summer

Small apples grow where
the blossoms used to be.
The apples get bigger and
tastier. Two hundred apples
may grow on one tree.

17

Picking fruit in autumn

In autumn, ripe apples are picked for selling.

Apple trees' leaves turn red and yellow

and fall to the ground.

The trees are bare. But branches

are covered with tight buds.

Apple trees in winter

Trees rest during cold months.
In spring, the buds open and
the life cycle begins again.

GLOSSARY

blossom flower on a fruit tree or other plant

bud small shoot on a plant that grows into a leaf or a flower

nectar sweet liquid found in many flowers

pollen powder made by flowers to help them create new seeds

ripe ready to pick and eat

root part of the plant that is underground

shoot white stem growing out of a seed that becomes a plant

stamen male part of the flower that makes pollen

FIND OUT MORE

BOOKS

Lifecycles (Ways into Science), Peter Riley (Franklin Watts, 2016)

The Amazing Plant Life Cycle Story, Kay Barnham (Wayland, 2017)

Trees (My First Book of Nature), Victoria Munson (Wayland, 2017)

WEBSITES

www.bbc.co.uk/education/clips/zf62tfr
Find out what happens to an apple tree through the seasons.

www.bbc.co.uk/education/clips/z3wsbk7
Learn about the life cycle of a plant in this video.

COMPREHENSION QUESTIONS

1. Why do bees fly from apple tree to apple tree?

2. We can see most parts of an apple tree.
   What part of an apple tree is under the ground?

INDEX